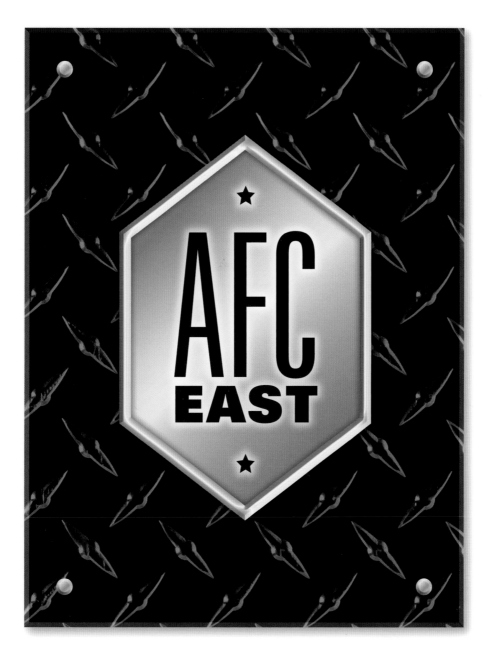

AFC EAST

BY K. C. KELLEY

★ Buffalo Bills ★ Miami Dolphins ★ New England Patriots ★ New York Jets ★

Published by The Child's World®
1980 Lookout Drive
Mankato, MN 56003-1705
800-599-READ
www.childsworld.com

The Child's World®: Mary Berendes, Publishing Director
The Design Lab: Kathleen Petelinsek, Design
Editorial Directions, Inc.: Pam Mamsch and E. Russell Primm,
Project Managers

Photographs ©: Robbins Photography

Copyright © 2012 by The Child's World®
All rights reserved. No part of this book may be reproduced or
utilized in any form or by any means without written permission
from the publisher.

Library of Congress Cataloging-in-Publication Data
Kelley, K. C.
  AFC East / by K. C. Kelley.
    p. cm. Includes bibliographical references and index.
  ISBN 978-1-60954-297-9 (library reinforced : alk. paper)
  1. National Football League—History—Juvenile literature.
  2. Football—United States—History—Juvenile literature. I. Title.
  GV955.5.N35K44 2011
   796.332'640973—dc22   2011007149

Printed in the United States of America
Mankato, MN
May, 2011
PA02093

TABLE OF
CONTENTS

AFC
EAST

4

First Season: 1960
AFL/NFL
  Championships: 2
Colors: Red, White,
and Blue
Mascot: Billy Buffalo

★

BUFFALO
BILLS

IT'S COLD . . . AND THEY LOVE IT!

The Buffalo Bills have to battle other great football teams, and they often have to take on the weather, too. The Bills play their home games in western New York. Winters are very cold, and it often snows. Bills fans bundle up and cheer with enthusiasm to keep warm!

The Bills started in the American Football League (AFL). The AFL was formed in 1960 to challenge the NFL, which had been around since 1920. The Bills won the AFL championship in 1964 and 1965. In 1970, AFL teams joined the NFL to form one big league. The Bills became part of the new American Football Conference (AFC).

The Bills played in and lost four straight Super Bowls (1990–93) after winning four AFC titles. Talk about cold! Today's Bills are hoping to return to the big game soon.

Running back Thurman Thomas helped the Bills win four AFC titles.

HOME FIELD

The Bills' home field is Ralph Wilson Stadium. It's named for the man who has owned the team since its first season in 1960. The team also plays one regular season game each year at the Rogers Centre in Toronto, Canada.

BIG DAYS

★ The Buffalo Bills won their first AFL championship in 1964. They defeated the San Diego Chargers 20–7.

★ Buffalo won its first AFC championship in 1990, beating Oakland 51–3. Then the Bills nearly won Super Bowl XXV. Kicker Scott Norwood just missed a last-play **field goal**, and the New York Giants won 20–19.

★ The Bills set a record in 1993 with their fourth straight AFC championship.

Ralph Wilson Stadium is in Orchard Park, New York.
It can hold more than 73,000 Bills fans.

SUPERSTARS!

★

THEN

Jim Kelly, quarterback: led Buffalo to four Super Bowls

Jack Kemp, quarterback: guided Bills to two AFL titles.

Bruce Smith, defensive end: NFL's all-time leader in **sacks** with 200

Thurman Thomas, running back: ran for more than
12,000 yards in NFL career

★

NOW

Ryan Fitzpatrick, quarterback: young and talented with a great future

Steve Johnson, wide receiver: connects well with Fitzpatrick downfield

C. J. Spiller, running back: another young player, great speed and moves

★

STAT LEADERS

(All-time team leaders*)

Passing Yards: Jim Kelly, 35,467

Rushing Yards: Thurman Thomas, 11,938

Receiving Yards: Andre Reed, 13,095

Touchdowns: Thurman Thomas and Andre Reed, 87

Interceptions: Butch Byrd, 40

★

(*Through 2010 season.)

TIMELINE

1960	1964	1965	1990
Buffalo Bills form as part of the new AFL.	Bills win AFL championship.	Bills win AFL championship.	Bills win AFC championship, lose Super Bowl XXV.

Jim Kelly was inducted into the Pro
Football Hall of Fame in 2002.

1991
Bills win AFC championship,
lose Super Bowl XXVI.

1992
Bills win AFC championship,
lose Super Bowl XXVII.

1993
Bills win AFC Championship
but lose Super Bowl XXVIII.

1999
Bills make playoffs as
wild-card team.

First Season: 1966
NFL Championships: 2
Colors: Aqua Green, Orange, and White
Mascot: T. D. the dolphin

★

MIAMI
DOLPHINS

A HOT TEAM FOR A HOT TOWN!

The greatest season in Dolphins history was also the greatest in NFL history. In 1972, just six seasons after their first season in 1966, the Dolphins won Super Bowl VII. On the way to that victory, they won every other game that season. Their 17–0 record is the only undefeated season in league history.

The Dolphins also had great seasons in the 1980s and early 1990s. They were led by rocket-armed passer Dan Marino. When he retired, he was the all-time leader in many passing stats.

The Dolphins made a lot of noise in 2008. The team's coaches created a new **formation** called the Wildcat. The ball was snapped to running back Ronnie Brown instead of the quarterback. The play fooled a lot of the Dolphins' opponents!

Jake Long was the Dolphins first round draft pick—and the first overall draft pick—in 2008.

HOME FIELD

Flags with the **retired numbers** of Dolphins greats fly above Sun Life Stadium. Built in 1987, it has been home to five Super Bowls!

BIG DAYS

★ Miami has the only undefeated season in NFL history. In 1972, they went 17–0. Then they capped off the season with a win in Super Bowl VII.
★ The Dolphins made it two championships in a row by beating the Minnesota Vikings in Super Bowl VIII.
★ Dan Marino set a record for passing yards during the 1984 season and led the Dolphins to the AFC championship.

Sun Life Stadium is in Miami Gardens, Florida. It can hold more than 75,000 football fans.

SUPERSTARS!

★

THEN

Larry Csonka, running back: bruising runner with a nose for the end zone
Dan Marino, quarterback: one of the greatest passers in NFL history
Don Shula, head coach: led team to two Super Bowl titles;
first all-time in NFL with 347 wins
Paul Warfield, wide receiver: great hands and the ability to get open

★

NOW

Ronnie Brown, running back: great runner who is also a great
pass catcher
Chad Henne, quarterback: young passer set to lead the Dolphins for years
Brandon Marshall, wide receiver: Pro Bowl player who
joined Miami in 2010

★

STAT LEADERS

(All-time team leaders*)
Passing Yards: Dan Marino, 61,361
Rushing Yards: Larry Csonka, 6,737
Receiving Yards: Mark Duper, 8,869
Touchdowns: Mark Clayton, 82
Interceptions: Jake Scott, 35

★

(*Through 2010 season.)

TIMELINE

1966
Dolphins' **expansion team** joins AFL.

1972
Dolphins win AFC title and Super Bowl VII; finish season undefeated.

1973
Dolphins win Super Bowl VIII.

Dan Marino was inducted into the Pro Football Hall of Fame in 2005.

1984

Dolphins win AFC title, lose Super Bowl XIX.

1987

Sun Life Stadium is built.

2000

Dolphins win AFC East championship.

First Season: 1960
NFL Championships: 3
Colors: Red, White, and Blue
Mascot: Pat Patriot

NEW ENGLAND
PATRIOTS

THEY LOVE THE 2000S!

The Patriots have played in two leagues. They've had two names. But they've had one goal—to win the championship! They've achieved that goal three times in the past decade.

The Patriots started in 1960 as the Boston Patriots in the AFL. In 1970, the Patriots and other AFL teams joined the NFL. In 1971, the team changed its name to the New England Patriots. For many years, the team did not have a lot of success.

That all changed in the new **millennium**. Since 2000, the Patriots have been one of the best teams in the NFL. Since 2001, they have been in four Super Bowls . . . and they have won three of them. What a great way to start a new century!

Linebacker Jerod Mayo was the Patriot's first round draft pick in 2008.

HOME FIELD

The Patriots play their home games at Gillette Stadium. It is in Foxborough, Massachusetts, which is west of Boston. Fans brave cold winter weather to cheer on their team. Each time the team scores, people dressed as **Minutemen** fire muskets to celebrate.

BIG DAYS

★ The Patriots played in their first Super Bowl after the 1985 season. They were the best team in the AFC. They lost that game to the Chicago Bears, 46–10.

★ The Patriots' first Super Bowl win was after the 2001 season. In one of the most exciting Super Bowls ever, they beat the St. Louis Rams 20–17. Kicker Adam Vinatieri made a 48-yard field goal on the last play of the game for the win.

★ Vinatieri did it again two years later. His 41-yard kick beat the Carolina Panthers in Super Bowl XXXVIII, 32–29.

More than 68,000 fans can pack Gillette Stadium to watch the Patriots play.

SUPERSTARS!

★

THEN

Nick Buoniconti, linebacker: hard-hitting tackler for the AFL Patriots
Steve Grogan, quarterback: led the Patriots to their first Super Bowl spot
John Hannah, guard: one of the best ever at his position
Mike Haynes, cornerback: outstanding at covering receivers

★

NOW

Bill Belichick, head coach: led the team to four Super Bowl appearances
Tom Brady, quarterback: led team to all three of its Super Bowl wins
Jerod Mayo, linebacker: a team leader in sacks and tackles
Wes Welker, receiver: small but brave, with great pass-catching hands

★

STAT LEADERS

(All-time team leaders*)
Passing Yards: Tom Brady, 34,744
Rushing Yards: Sam Cunningham, 5,453
Receiving Yards: Stanley Morgan, 10,352
Touchdowns: Stanley Morgan, 68
Interceptions: Ty Law and Raymond Clayborn, 36

★

(*Through 2010 season.)

TIMELINE

Wel Welker had a team-record
123 receptions in 2009.

22

First Season: 1960
AFL/NFL
    Championships: 1
Colors: Green and
    White
Mascot: None

NEW YORK

JETS

ARE THESE JETS READY FOR TAKEOFF?

When the AFL started in 1960, the league's team in New York was called the Titans. They wore blue-and-gold uniforms. In 1963, the team changed its name to the Jets and its colors to green and white. In 1968, led by famous quarterback Joe Namath, the Jets were the first team from the AFL to win a Super Bowl.

The Jets had some good seasons in the 1980s and 1990s, but they haven't been back to the Super Bowl since Namath's time.

Head coach Rex Ryan took over the Jets in 2009, and things are looking up. With a super-tough defense and an offense led by **rookie** quarterback Mark Sanchez, they made it to the AFC Championship game. Looks like the Jets are ready to start flying again!

Quarterback Mark Sanchez was the Jets' first round draft pick in 2009.

HOME FIELD

The Jets got a brand-new home in 2010. The New Meadowlands Stadium is actually in New Jersey, not New York. It's also home to the New York Giants. The stadium will be the site of the Super Bowl in 2014, the first for the New York City area.

BIG DAYS

★ Namath "guaranteed" that his team would **upset** the Colts in Super Bowl III. He came through with a 16–7 win for the Jets. The game is one of the most famous in NFL history.
★ Under former Giants coach Bill Parcells, the Jets set a team record with 12 wins in 1998. They made it to the AFC Championship Game.
★ Though they won only nine games during the regular season, the Jets made it to the 2009 AFC Championship Game.

New Meadowlands Stadium is located in East Rutherford, New Jersey. It seats more than 82,000 fans.

SUPERSTARS!

★

THEN

Curtis Martin, running back: team all-time and 2004 NFL rushing leader

Don Maynard, wide receiver: small and quiet, but made tons of key catches

Joe Namath, quarterback: rocket-armed passer and popular hero

★

NOW

Antonio Cromartie, cornerback: terrific at covering receivers, nose for the ball

Mark Sanchez, quarterback: as rookie, led team to AFC title game

LaDainian Tomlinson, running back: former San Diego star got new life as a Jet

★

STAT LEADERS

(All-time team leaders*)

Passing Yards: Joe Namath, 27,057

Rushing Yards: Curtis Martin, 10,302

Receiving Yards: Don Maynard, 11,732

Touchdowns: Don Maynard, 88

Interceptions: Bill Baird, 34

★

(*Through 2010 season.)

TIMELINE

1960
New York AFL team, called the Titans, is created.

1963
Team changes its name to Jets.

1968
Jets surprise many people and win Super Bowl III over the Colts.

Joe Namath was inducted into the Pro Football Hall of Fame in 1985.

1998
Jets earn a spot in the AFC Championship Game.

2009
Jets battle through the playoffs to reach the AFC title game.

2010
Jets begin playing home games at New Meadowlands Stadium.

STAT
STUFF

★

AFC EAST DIVISION STATISTICS*

Team	All-Time Record (W-L-T)	NFL Titles (Most Recent)	Times in NFL Playoffs
Buffalo Bills	372–421–8	2 (1965)	17
Miami Dolphins	414–310–4	2 (1973)	22
New England Patriots	422–377–9	3 (2005)	18
New York Jets	363–426–8	1 (1968)	14

★

AFC EAST DIVISION CHAMPIONSHIPS
(MOST RECENT)

Buffalo Bills . . . 7 (1995)

Miami Dolphins . . . 13 (2008)

New England Patriots . . . 12 (2010)

New York Jets . . . 2 (2002)

★

(*Through 2010 season; includes AFL statistics.)

AFC EAST PRO FOOTBALL
HALL OF FAME MEMBERS

Buffalo Bills

Joe DeLamielleure, G
Jim Kelly, QB
Marv Levy, coach
James Lofton, WR
Billy Shaw, G
O. J. Simpson, RB
Bruce Smith, DE
Thurman Thomas, RB
Ralph Wilson, Jr., owner

Miami Dolphins

Nick Buoniconti, LB
Larry Csonka, RB
Bob Griese, QB
Jim Langer, C
Larry Little, C
Dan Marino, QB
Don Shula, coach
Dwight Stephenson, C
Paul Warfield, WR

New England Patriots

Nick Buoniconti, LB
John Hannah, G
Mike Haynes, CB
Andre Tippett, LB

New York Jets

Weeb Ewbank, coach
Don Maynard, WR
Joe Namath, QB
John Riggins, RB

NOTE: Includes players with at least three seasons with team. Players may appear with more than one team.

Position Key:
QB: Quarterback
RB: Running back
WR: Wide receiver
C: Center
T: Tackle
G: Guard
CB: Cornerback
LB: Linebacker
DE: Defensive end

GLOSSARY

★

expansion team (ek-SPAN-shuhn TEEM): new team added to an existing league

field goal (FEELD GOHL): a kick that starts from the field and goes between the uprights; worth three points

formation (for-MAY-shuhn): the way that teams line up on the football field

millennium (muh-LEN-ee-uhm): a period of 1,000 years

Minutemen (MIN-it-men): American soldiers in the Revolutionary War; they got their name from being able to be "ready to fight in a minute"

retired numbers (rih-TIRED NUHM-burz): jersey numbers that will never be used again; done to honor great players

rookie (ROOK-ee): a player in his first pro sports season

sacks (SAKSS): tackles made on the quarterback behind where his team started with the ball

upset (UP-set): in sports, a victory by a team or player not expected to win

FIND OUT MORE

★

BOOKS

Buckley, James. *Scholastic Ultimate Guide to Football*. New York: Franklin Watts, 2009.

MacRae, Sloan. *The Miami Dolphins*. New York: PowerKids Press, 2011.

MacRae, Sloan. *The New England Patriots*. New York: PowerKids Press, 2011.

Stewart, Mark. *The Buffalo Bills*. Chicago: Norwood House Press, 2008.

Stewart, Mark. *The New York Jets*. Chicago: Norwood House Press, 2010.

★

WEB SITES

For links to learn more about football visit
www.childsworld.com/links

Note to Parents, Teachers, and Librarians: We routinely verify our Web links to make sure they are safe and active sites. So encourage your readers to check them out!

INDEX

ABOUT THE AUTHOR

K. C. Kelley has written dozens of books about sports for young readers, including several on football. He used to work for the NFL and has covered several Super Bowls. He helped start NFL.com and still watches games every Sunday all season long!